THE SOURCE OF EVERYDAY THINGS

Illustrated by Aldren Watson

Platt & Munk, Publishers/New York

PAPER

Paper comes from trees. To make paper, trees are chopped down. The logs are fed into a drum that turns quickly, peeling off the bark. Then the bare logs are carried along a conveyor belt to a chipper. There they are chopped into tiny pieces.

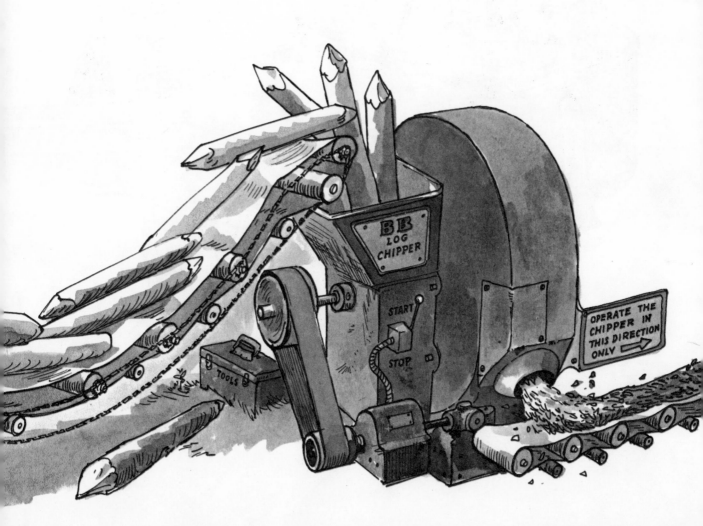

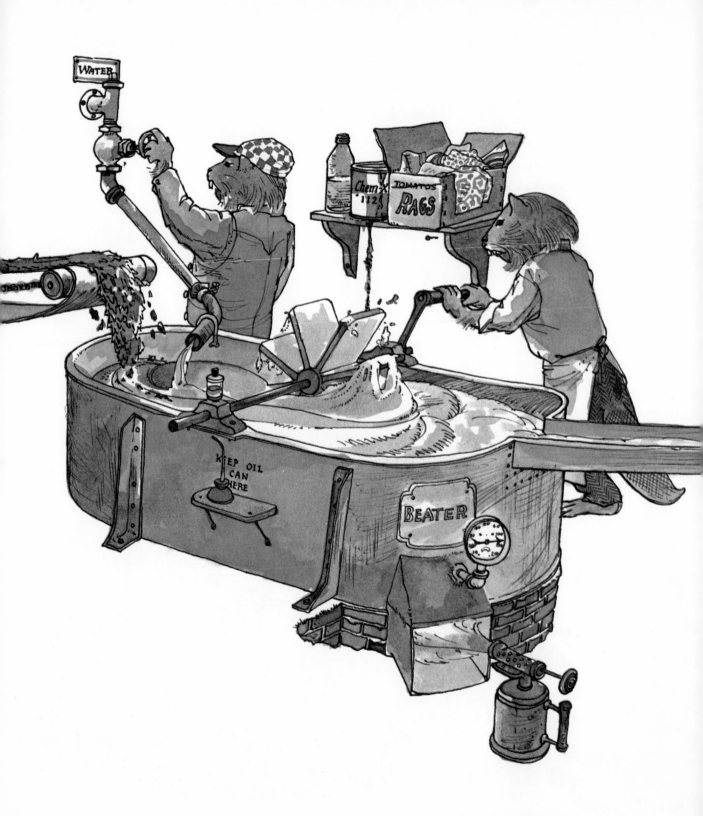

The wood chips are mashed until they have become soggy. This soggy wood is called *pulp*. To the pulp are added chemicals and even rags. The mixture is cooked until all the chemicals have set. Then it is poured over a fine screen so that the excess water can drip out.

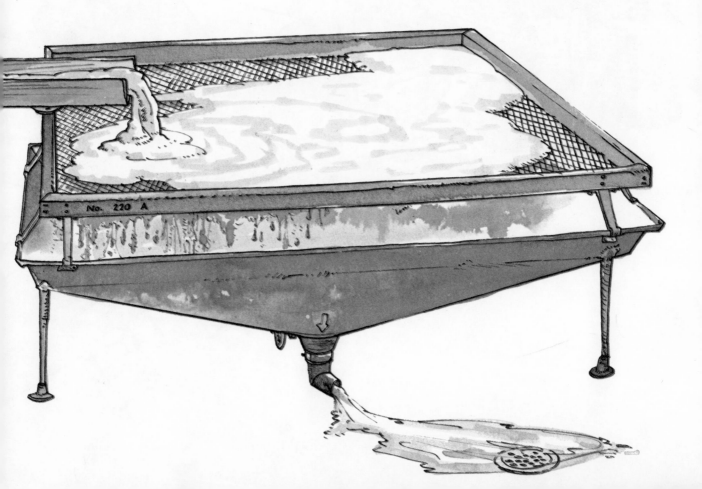

Next, the pulp is pressed between huge rollers to make it thin and flat. While the paper is passing through the rollers, heaters blow it dry. When it reaches the end of the rollers, the flat, dry paper is wound around tubes into huge rolls. The paper is carried away to plants which use it to make books and magazines and newspapers.

PAINT

The color in paint comes from pigment. Pigment is the coloring substance in the cells and tissues of natural matter. Red pigment comes from a mineral in the earth. Purple comes from a seashell called *murex*. Blue comes from a plant called *indigo*. And reddish-brown comes from a fish called a *cuttlefish*.

INDIGO PLANT (BLUE)

EARTH (RED)

CUTTLEFISH (BROWN)

MUREX (PURPLE)

The material from which the pigment is taken
is ground into a fine powder at the paint factory.
Then chemicals are added to it. Linseed oil is
added to hold the paint together. A thinner, like
turpentine, is added to keep it from being too thick.

And a drier is added to help the paint dry
quickly. Everything is whirled together, and then
the paint is put into cans and tubes. The cans and
tubes are carried away to stores.

COTTON CLOTH

Cotton cloth comes from a plant with a fluffy ball of fiber growing on its top. A cotton picking machine picks the fluffy balls and places them in a cage. The fluffy balls are taken to the cotton gin. The cotton gin is a machine that separates the seeds from the fluff, or cotton. The cotton is cleaned, and then it is packed in bales and sent to the spinner.

The spinner puts the cotton on a machine with sticks like fork prongs that twist the cotton onto the spinning wheel. The spinning wheel spins the cotton into thread.

The thread is wound onto spools and sent off to the weaver. The weaver places the thread on a loom and weaves long bolts of material. The bolts of cotton cloth are carried away to clothing factories and stores.

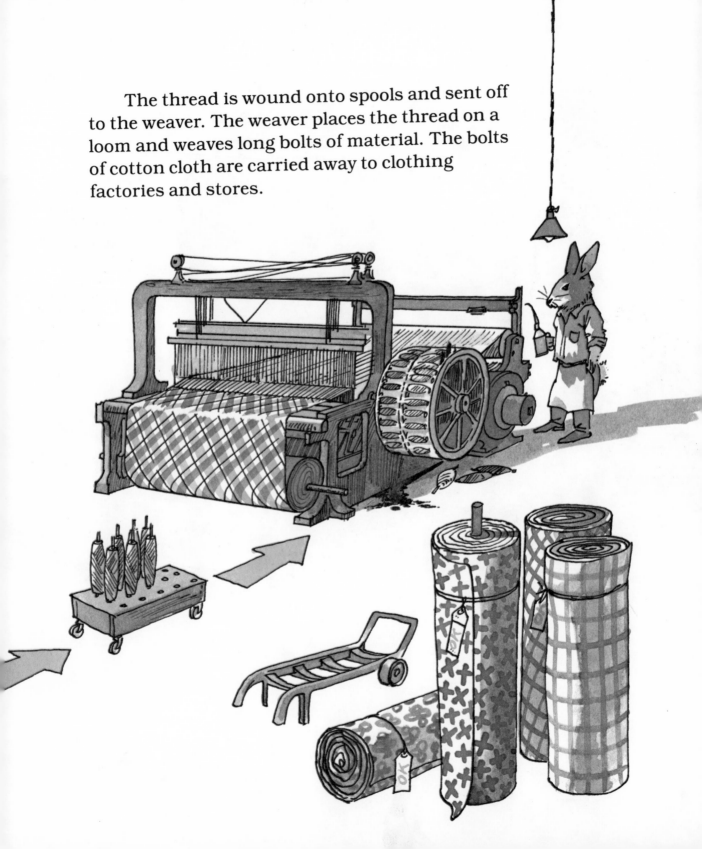

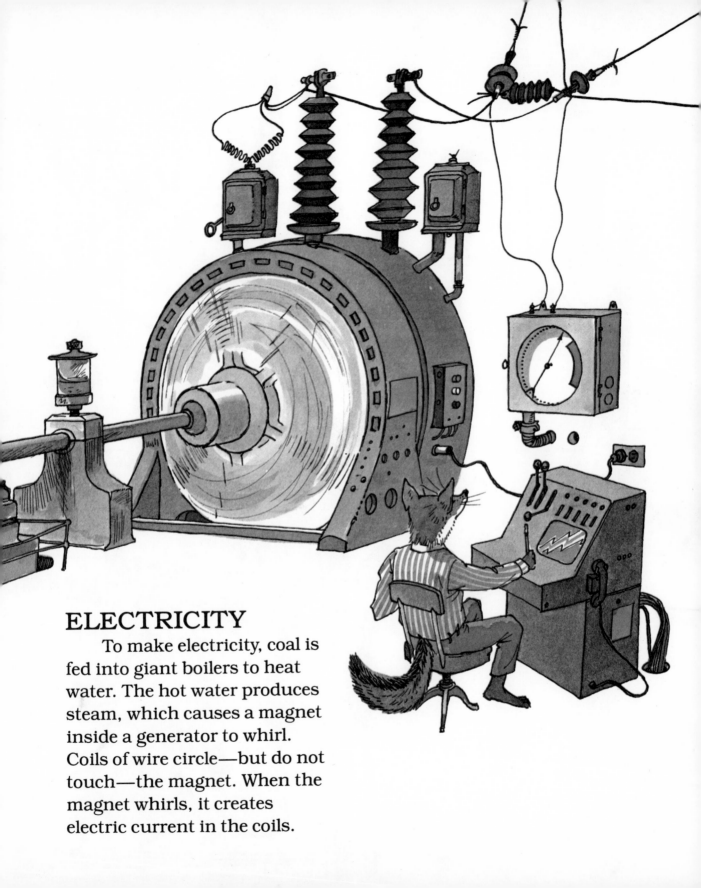

ELECTRICITY

To make electricity, coal is fed into giant boilers to heat water. The hot water produces steam, which causes a magnet inside a generator to whirl. Coils of wire circle—but do not touch—the magnet. When the magnet whirls, it creates electric current in the coils.

The electric current travels from the generator into huge wires that run underground or above ground on poles, carrying the electricity to all buildings which use it. Inside each of these buildings are smaller wires that carry the electricity to every room.

FRUITS AND VEGETABLES

Fruits and vegetables come from farms. Each year, the farmer saves seeds from his crop. In the spring, he plants the seeds in the ground in long rows. Every day, he waters the seeds and makes sure there are no weeds to rob them of nutrients and sunshine. The plants grow all summer long.

In the autumn, the farmer goes out to the fields with his truck, ladder, and bushel baskets. He places the ladder against the fruit trees and climbs up to gather the ripe fruits. He picks all the fruits and vegetables, separating them into bushel baskets. Then he loads the baskets onto his truck and carries them away to market.